GOD
IS MY BIGGEST FAN

❧✿❧

How Grace and Mercy Blessed My Life

SHARON A. WRIGHT

ISBN 978-1-0980-5660-5 (paperback)
ISBN 978-1-0980-5661-2 (digital)

Copyright © 2020 by Sharon A. Wright

All rights reserved. No part of this publication may be reproduced, distributed, or transmitted in any form or by any means, including photocopying, recording, or other electronic or mechanical methods without the prior written permission of the publisher. For permission requests, solicit the publisher via the address below.

Christian Faith Publishing, Inc.
832 Park Avenue
Meadville, PA 16335
www.christianfaithpublishing.com

Printed in the United States of America

This book is dedicated in loving memory of
my mom and dad, Cynthia and Charlie.
May your souls continue to rest peacefully in paradise!
Until we meet again!

Love forever and always,
your daughter, Sharon

Dear Joyce,

Thank you for supporting me & always being so encouraging!

Love,
Sharon

Give *thanks* unto the LORD, call upon His name,
make known His deeds among the people.

—1 Chronicles 16:8 (KJV)

Contents

Foreword 9

Thoughts of Gratitude 11

Introduction 13

The Innocence of a Child 15

Looking for Love in All the Wrong Places 18

When Times Are Hard 23

Growing Pains 25

Does My Special Someone Exist? 29

The Love of My Life 35

Instant Family 41

Overcoming the Enemy 44

Finding and Loving Me 48

Sometimes You Need a Push 51

GOD's Love Is the Prize 54

Heartfelt Gratitude 56

Foreword

When my mom told me she was writing a book, I couldn't believe it. I had no idea she had been working on a book. I first wondered what it was about, then if I would be in it. You can only imagine how shocked I was when she asked me to write something for her! I felt honored but more nervous than anything. What would I say? She ended up giving me a snippet to read, and I can honestly say that I'm so proud of my mom. I always knew she was a strong person but after reading that, I admired her strength so much more. Of course, I shed a few tears, but it gave me a different view of my mother. You know how they say you never really know your parents? I've always believed it to be true. I learned a few things about my mom, her life before me. I'm beyond grateful that she's allowed me to see another side of her. It really makes you appreciate your parents so much more.

The snippet my mom gave me is titled "Love of My Life." Who could that possibly be? Come to find out it was about me. I never really knew how much I meant to my mom. The complete impact I had on her life. She's been my entire world, like the best mom you could ask for. She's sacrificed so much for me, overcame a lot of struggles, and for that, she will always be my inspiration. No, she's not perfect, no parent is, but for her to be a single parent while going through life's obstacles, protecting me along the way, I say she's pretty close to it. I had everything I needed from birth to this day. Even my wants were fulfilled. I can remember asking for something and she would tell me "no," but I'd always end up getting it. Some may say I'm spoiled; I just think I'm blessed to have someone so selfless and kindhearted. I thank GOD every day for my mother. I can see a lot of her in me, so I can't wait to read the entire book and continue learning about her life. I know how much this book means to my mom and that it'll touch a lot of people, so I hope everyone who reads it enjoys it!

Love,
Tatyana
Proud Daughter

Thoughts of Gratitude

First and foremost, I have to give my thanks to the Creator for bringing me to this moment because I know that without GOD, I would not be here today. I am so grateful!

My daughter, Tatyana. I have learned so much about life through our mother-daughter relationship, and for that, I am forever grateful that GOD chose me to by your mother.

My siblings whom I have been through some hard times and great times with that have made us who we are today. GOD put us together as a family for a reason, and I'm grateful for each and every one of you. The six of you have taught me various lessons throughout my life, and I only hope that I have done the same. I love you!

My life partner who has always believed in me from the start. Thank you for always having words of encouragement to keep me focused on my path. I know I don't say it enough, but you motivate me to be the best version of myself, and for that, I am grateful.

My lifelong friends, it always amazes me how we can get together and erase time. We have been friends for over forty years, and there is nothing that will change the fact that I love each and every one of you like family. I am grateful that GOD put you in my life when He did. #BG4Life

My teachers, I had some great teachers throughout my matriculation through grade school, middle and high schools, and college. Some of them taught me reading, math, science, and general studies courses. Others taught me how to be a good person who respected herself and others. I will forever be grateful to each of them for accepting the call to inspire and mold young minds!

My therapist, Ms. Victoria, who was new to my life in 2017. I was scared in the beginning because I had no idea how to open up and share the issues of my life. She made me comfortable and just started talking to me like a human being. I am grateful she was able to help me break down the walls of my shame and embarrassment to find me standing on the other side. I will always be grateful to your listening ear and empathetic heart. Thank you!

My guardian angels, Mom, Dad, and Grandmothers. I would not exist if they never existed. We went through so much in the short time we had together, but each relationship made an impression on my life. I was angry through some of it, but I never stopped loving any of you and never will. It's great to know that you are all together watching over me and the family. I am completely grateful for the life lessons! May you continue to rest in paradise! I love you!

My readers, I am grateful that you decided to pick up my very first book and give it a chance to bless your life. It is my hope that you will allow my story to inspire your story.

Thank you!

Finally, I want to recognize the one person in my life that would not give up or give in to the nightmares, the negative self-talk, and years of broken-heartedness, me. I was broken early in my life but GOD! I was hurt by many but GOD! I stumbled many times but GOD! I am truly grateful that GOD made me, because without me, this book would not exist. Thank You, GOD!

Introduction

I was not raised in the church, but I went to church once in a while with a family friend and with my grandmother and an aunt while visiting them in Savannah, Georgia, for the summer breaks. I actually loved going to church and getting all dressed up on Easter and Christmas.

Although I was not a full-fledged member of any particular church, I always believed in GOD and Jesus Christ. I believed at an early age that there was this being that watched over us and listened to our prayers. I believed that He blessed our food and our homes and all the people we prayed for at night before we went to bed.

I believed that GOD created the sun, the moon, and the stars. I believed He created the trees, animals, and each one of us. I believed that I would be forgiven for hitting my sister or talking about someone I didn't even know. I believed that GOD gave me my freckles, my colorful hair, my light-colored skin, and my siblings on purpose! I believed all these things at a very early age, and I still believe them, even more so today.

I wrote this book because I am at the point in my life where I can accept my relationship with the Creator is the most important relationship I will ever have with anyone. I wanted to share the experiences in my life that I had no control over but made it out of with my life still intact because of GOD's grace and mercy. Please know that this book was not written with the intent to hurt or harm anyone but for me to let go of the past and focus on where I am right now. I want to release the pain and hurt through my testimonies so that they become butterflies in someone else's life.

I am inspired by the testimonies of others whether I hear it in church or when a singer is testifying of GOD's blessings upon her/his life through song. I feel so touched by these testimonies that they bring me to tears sometimes. As human beings, we are tested daily, but it's how we deal with these tests that make the difference. Do we just ball up in a knot and cry our eyes out? Do we fall on our knees and ask for Heavenly Father's guidance? When we do the latter, even if after the first, we find that it was only a test and GOD helped us through it because we asked Him for help. It is my hope that you read my life stories of GOD's grace and mercy through some very pivotal moments in my life and feel inspired to bear your testimony to someone who is waiting to hear from the Lord. We must remember that we are mere vessels of GOD's message to our brothers and sisters. Be ready to share your story; it just might save someone's life.

Writing this book or putting my life story in writing has been very cathartic. So much so that I finally faced a big fear of mine, therapy. I could feel the chains of the past falling off me. I am *free*! I am no longer held hostage by the hurt, anger, and anguish of yesteryears! I can finally spread my wings and fly to the highest heights GOD always intended for me.

I am so thrilled to share this book with you and look forward to allowing you to see what the future brings to my life. Whatever you may be wrestling with, I want you to practice forgiveness of others and especially yourself. Forgive those that caused your life any distress and forgive yourself for believing that any of it was your fault. Pray for GOD's grace and mercy in your life and it shall be given unto you. Amen!

The Innocence of a Child

Lo, *children* are an heritage of the LORD:
And the fruit of the womb is His reward.

—Psalm 27:3

I have many memories of my childhood, happy and sad. The memory that I want to release from my long-term memory bank is the one that started it all as far as GOD's grace and mercy. It's the memory that has held me hostage for too long!

I had to be around eight years old when it happened. I did not understand what was happening nor why it was happening. Please understand that I am sharing my testimony of this moment in my life not to hurt anyone but to demonstrate how GOD can take your enemies and use them as footstools in your life. GOD can take a horrible experience and turn it into a victory for you.

So as I was sleeping in a bed I shared with my younger sister, my breathing suddenly became constricted. I had no idea what was happening to me. Why did I feel such pressure on my chest? Why couldn't I breathe? I thought I was dreaming and started to wake up. As I awakened to stop this horrible dream, I realized I was not dreaming.

I soon learned that I couldn't breathe because someone was on my back grinding on me. They were much heavier than me, which explained the constriction I felt in my chest.

I was coming out of my sleep and started to move around which ran the person off. I was young, so I wasn't sure what was going on.

I was highly confused and devastated at the same time. I did not understand why this person would want to cause me any harm. I was a child, an innocent child.

This happened several more times before it ended. I began sleeping with my backside to the wall to discourage this person from trying this ever again. I also started to move around a lot whenever it was bedtime because I was sharing the bed with my sister, and I did not want anything to happen to her. I hope she understands why I never shared this with her; I just wanted to protect her and the relationship she had with this person.

I was afraid to tell my mother what was going on. I believed she would blame me for it. I was scared, embarrassed, and heartbroken. I had no one that I could talk to about what was happening to me. My relationship with my mom (even at that young age) was not the greatest. I sometimes felt like I did not belong to my family. I could not bring myself to tell her.

I remember hiding in our bedroom closet and crying silently. I wanted to understand why this thing happened to me. I asked GOD, "Why did this have to happen to me?" There was no response. I cried many days about this without any answers. I wanted to die. This was the first time I felt like that.

I never told my mom or any of my siblings what happened to me. I wanted to just forget about it and move on with my life. Who knew it would come back to haunt me as an adult. I would see television shows where women are revealing how they were sexually molested, raped, and violated. It had me in tears. I knew I needed to tell someone. I had to release this negative energy from my life because it still had a hold on me.

I was having anxiety attacks and bouts of depression. I would start crying at the drop of a dime. This had to stop! So I told one person that I had been molested as a child. I still haven't revealed the identity of the person who could do such an awful thing to a young child, but it was out. He held me as I cried, and I felt better.

I believe GOD placed him in my life at that particular time to give me the opportunity to be free from this unfortunate event. He is the only person I have ever spoken with directly about what happened to me. This gave him a better understanding of why I acted in certain ways.

GOD is not the only force in this world, and I never blamed Him for what happened to me. I realized years later that this happened to prevent this person from doing it to anyone else. GOD uses us to protect others that may not be able to deal with that same situation in the manner in which you did. Although this was a miserable moment in my life, I am stronger because of it. I am grateful that GOD's grace taught me this lesson and His mercy helps me deal with the memory of it in a more positive way.

It is my testimony that if you continue to pray and have faith, GOD will bring you out of any situation. I was a child and had my innocence stolen from me, but because of who my Father is, I lived through it. I am able to share my story with you because GOD said it's time for me to let it go. I'm letting it go and moving on to live the life my Heavenly Father intended for me to live all along. I am a child of GOD and born of royalty. It's time for me to take control of my life by forgiving the violator and healing that little girl who still lives inside of me. She is no longer a victim but a survivor! I am not a victim! GOD's love prevails overall. I can only praise Him for keeping me long enough to know that it was never my fault. I committed no crime and did not deserve the punishment I put myself through for so many years.

Thank You, GOD, for guiding me to this moment, for giving me the strength and courage to finally release these bad feelings. I condemned myself for a crime I didn't commit but was too scared to tell anyone. I forgive myself. I forgive him. I just want to move on.

Looking for Love in All the Wrong Places

> Beloved, let us *love* one another: for love is of GOD;
> And every one that loveth is born of GOD, and knoweth GOD.
>
> —1 John 4:7

If you have not been the victim of molestation or some other sex crime, it's probably hard for you to understand the things we put ourselves through afterward. Your expectations of love are skewed, and you think love is everything that it's not. This is the hardest chapter to write because I have to be open and honest with myself about how I treated my body. I did not love myself. I did not believe I deserved to be loved the right way.

After what happened to me as a young girl, as a teenager I expected boys to only want sex from me. My first time was at age fifteen with someone I thought I was in love with. I thought he loved me too. How wrong I was! This was the beginning of some of the worst moments of my life.

One particular relationship came about when I was eighteen. I met this guy whom I thought was really nice and he was cute. We started dating and hanging out together all the time. I knew his brother from school and believed he was a good guy because his brother was really nice. What I found out later was that I could not have been more wrong.

He was always doing sweet things for me. He would come by and bring me gifts like stuffed animals, tennis shoes, clothes, and flowers. I remember for Valentine's Day, he bought me this huge stuffed teddy bear with balloons and flowers. My mom could not stand him. She would always ask me how he could buy me so much stuff. I would just tell her that he had a job, and he did have a job. Just not one she would approve of.

How do you tell your mother that your new boyfriend is a hustler, a drug dealer? It was hard to get away from them; they were everywhere in my neighborhood. Besides, she knew. She would make remarks like, "He better not bring any drugs in my house!" We would get into it all the time over this boyfriend of mine. As if we needed anything else to put a wedge between us.

There was an instance when he asked me to hold some drugs for him. We argued about it, and I told him that my mother would lose her mind if she ever found drugs in her house. He convinced me that she would never know and that I would not have to hold it for long. So he brought a safe with the drugs inside and hid it in my sister's and my closet. We covered it with clothes and other things to keep it out of view from anyone that might go into the closet.

The drugs ended up staying in our closet for a few weeks until my mother found out about it. I was scared to death when she found the safe in the closet. She told me I better get that mess (of course she used a more explicit term) out of her house. This thing was heavy. I had the hardest time moving it. I pushed it under the steps in the hallway outside our door. I called him and told him he had to come to get it but not to let my mother see him.

I was terrified that someone would find it. I also worried that my mother would put me out for disobeying her. What can I say? I thought I was grown. After a horrible exchange of words with my mother, I left with him. He didn't have a place of his own, so we checked in to a motel and stayed there for a couple of weeks. A friend of his and his girlfriend stayed with us. Let me just say there was a lot of sex happening in that room. We would go shopping, eat out at restaurants, and just hang out all day long. I thought this was the life! Boy was I wrong.

After two weeks of bliss or what I thought was bliss, I started to see the evilness in his eyes. He was very controlling and obsessive. He thought I wanted to get with his friend which was far from the truth. Here I was thinking we were falling in love and I had fallen into the abyss of an abusive relationship. He dropped me off blocks away from home. Needless to say, I called my mother and begged her forgiveness so I could come back home.

I did not see or hear from him for a long time. I found out that he had been locked up. Next thing I know, I get a phone call from him saying he was returning from California and wanted to see me. I agreed to see him. We were going out for dinner and a movie. I had to meet him outside because if my mother knew it was him that I was going out with, she would be extremely upset.

He showed up at my house driving a car that had my name on the doors. Red flags! I was naive and felt flattered. We started out for our date. He then said he needed to stop by his grandmother's house for something. I was cool with that, so we went to her house. Here comes another red flag. We entered the house from the back and went straight to his room which was in an area like an attic but had a door and stairs that led outside at the back of the house.

So we got in there and I was just standing there waiting for him to get whatever he came for. He started hugging up on me and telling me how much he missed me and wanted me back. I was like, come on, let's go. Sirens are going off at this point! Well, things escalated, and he grabbed me, threw me on the bed, and tried to take my pants off. I kept telling him to get off me. I tried to scream out to whoever was downstairs. He put his hand over my mouth. This was a nightmare!

I was kicking and scratching as I attempted to get away from him. I told him I did not want that and I wanted to go home. He continued trying until I was crying uncontrollably. He got off me and apologized. I continue to cry and fix my clothes. When we were on our way back to the car, I tried to run away. He caught me, grabbed me, and slammed me on the trunk of someone's car. He told me not to run from him again. I agreed. I just wanted to go home and get as far away from him as possible.

We got into his car with me still crying like crazy. He apologized again. As we were on our way back to my house, he pulled into an alley and stopped the car. I asked, "What are you doing?" He started trying to explain to me how much he loves me and wants to be with me. I just kept saying that I wanted to go home. He told me to get out of the car. I complied. We were standing at the back of the car, and he was still pleading with me to calm down and understand that he loves me and wants to be with me.

So here we were in this dark alley only God knows where. My mind was racing, trying to figure out how I could get myself out of this. I started to run toward the street leading to the alley. The next thing I heard was his voice telling me to come back or he would shoot me. I knew he went into the trunk for something, but I had no idea that it was a gun. When I turned around, I saw the gun in his hand. I started walking back to him. He told me to get in the car which I did. I was crying so hard that I was about to throw up. I could not talk or do anything but cry. He finally started the car, and we were moving again.

I did not know where we were going, but I pleaded with him to take me home. I told him that I would not tell anyone about what happened if he would just take me home. He apologized profusely and took me home. He sat there until he thought I went into the apartment. I didn't.

I could not go into my mother's house looking the way I looked after such a traumatic event. When he pulled off, I left the building and went to a friend's house down the street but in the same complex. I needed to go somewhere to get myself together before I went home because my mother and brothers would lose it. They would want to go after this guy and beat the life out of him or have him locked up. I just wanted it to be over.

I stayed at my friend's place until I was calm and feeling better. They took me in and comforted me. I never told them exactly what had happened to me. I just said that we had a fight. I was embarrassed and ashamed yet again.

I finally went home and no one ever knew what went down that day until now. I was and still am grateful for Heavenly Father bringing me out of that situation with my life intact. I had never been so scared or felt so close to death as I did that night. I still cry about it because I did not know what I had done to deserve such ugliness in my life. I know without a doubt that the angels, grace, and mercy were with me that night in that room and in that alley. I was absolutely terrified that he was going to kill us both in that alley. But GOD!

It is my testimony that without GOD's divine and unconditional love, I would not be here right now sharing this with the world. GOD allowed me to live through that horrible moment to be a blessing to someone else who has a story like this they have yet to share with anyone. It is my testimony that this moment in time taught me to pay attention to the signs, the red flags that the universe is sending me. My name on the car doors after not seeing or speaking with him for almost a year was a warning. Pay attention, ladies; GOD is trying to tell you something! Be wary of looking for love in all the wrong places. Thank You, GOD, for bringing me through and out of that terrifying moment in my life.

When Times Are Hard

(original poem © 1994)

When life deals you a crappy hand
You feel you cannot play
Take time out of your busy schedule
To get on your knees and pray

Wake up and open your eyes
Be thankful to see the sunrise
Don't let the devil psyche you out
Just show him what your GOD's all about

Sometimes the road to a successful life
Can seem like a distant friend
But you have to keep your head held high
And know that you can win

Think about what Jesus did for you
He put His life on the line
So put your enemies behind you
And say, "Sweet victory shall be mine!"

This original poem was written when I was away at college after the passing of my dear mother. I was in the computer lab working on an assignment. I started thinking about her, and the words just began flowing from my heart to the page. GOD only knows how much I miss her. I think about her every day from the moment I wake until I go to sleep. Ma, I love you eternally and I know we'll be together again, but until then, I hope I'm making you proud. It's all I ever wanted in this life.

Growing Pains

> For by *grace* are ye saved through faith;
> And that not of yourselves: it is the gift of *GOD*.
>
> —Ephesians 2:8

Where do I even begin? I remember the various stages of my life as a little girl. I can see myself when I was around two or three. I have flashes of me when I was between the ages of five to ten. And of course, I have memories of me as a teenager. For as early as I can remember, I have always felt like a stranger in my family. Primarily because I did not look like everyone else.

My parents were of darker hues than me; Mom was like milk chocolate and Dad was more like dark chocolate. Then came this little girl who was lighter than them both. I heard stories about my complexion that did not make things better for me. My own family made fun of me because of the color of my skin. So much so that I thought I was adopted.

There was a lot of pain in my childhood just because of my lighter complexion. I never really talked about it with anyone. As you can tell, I was not big on sharing how I felt about anything, especially things that hurt me. I kept this close to the chest as well. Not anymore. It is time to release it all so I can heal all the wounds that have held me hostage for too many years. Breathe.

I am not sure why others felt the need to talk about my complexion almost every time I saw them, but they did. I built such a complex about it that I did not like the skin I was in. I could not understand what the big deal was! It was just skin! There were stories about my mother sleeping with some Caucasian man. As if this were funny! *Not*! I may have smiled and grinned in their presence, but when I was alone, I cried.

I cried because I did not know who I was or why I was chosen to be the lighter-skinned child in my family. I cried because they had hurt my feelings. I loved my mother and my father and didn't want to hear those ugly stories anymore. I cried because I just wanted to belong. No one knew the pain I felt when they talked about my complexion. No one bothered to ask me how I felt either. So I cried alone and buried my true feelings deep down inside myself.

The older I became, the more I tried to solve the mystery. I questioned whether my dad was really my dad. I wondered, if he was not my real dad, where was my real dad? Did he know about me and did not want me? Who is he? Didn't I have a right to know the truth? These questions went unanswered because I hid them in that special place within me. I dare not say them out loud. The fear of what would happen to me if I did ask was enough to keep me quiet.

There were other things I was teased about growing up as the fifth out of six children. Mom and Dad separated when I was very young, but I remember when they were together. Things were great from my toddler perspective. I was happy! Happy until I wasn't. Why is it that your family hurts you more than strangers in the world? I'm sure it's because you care about what they say more than some random person.

I used to wonder how I could feel so lonely in a house full of people. That's genuinely how I felt in my family. I tell people all the time that I was a loner growing up. Yes, there were times when I hung out with my family and friends and had great times. However, there were a lot of times when I would be present but absent at the same time. I would just go off into my own little world.

Please don't get me wrong, I love my family, my siblings. I just constantly felt like an outsider though. I tried to find ways to erase that feeling but it would not go away. I did not know it then but I know now that I have been suffering from depression since I was eight years old. I never even considered that to be a possibility. I just thought I was different. Unique. Depression? Nah!

I wish this was something I knew back then because I could have received help. I believe in my heart of hearts that if I had the help I needed back then, things would be much different today and even back then. My relationship with my mother is one thing I know for sure would have been different. Better. We had some special moments together, and we had some moments that were rocky.

My mom was raising six children on her own. She did the best she could with what she had. Dad was not around that much. He spent more time with my younger sister and me during the early years. But Mom, she was always there. I am not sure why we bumped heads so much. Probably because we were so much alike and different at the same time.

She would hurt my feelings when she called out my name, blame me for something I didn't do. I would defy her sometimes because I felt like I would be yelled at or hit anyway so I might as well have fun while I could.

This is a warped way of thinking. A warped way of living and having a relationship with a parent. I wanted us to be close. I envied the relationship my mom had with my youngest sister. I wanted that to be us and just when things were turning around for us, she was gone. I cannot express how deep this hurt was and still is today.

This is my testimony of love. GOD loves us unconditionally. He loves us despite our transgressions, flaws, scars, inabilities, and all that stuff. GOD wants us to love one another in the same manner. When I lost my mother, my world came crashing in on me. Time's up! I had no say so in that matter. It was just done. I wanted to get back all those lost moments to talk with her about how I was feeling at the different stages in my life up until that time. We were getting along much better at the time of her transition. That's because I was out on my own, working, and taking care of myself. I would go by to see her after work or on my days off. She would call me and ask me to bring her something, and I was happy to do it. She was my mom, and I loved her, still do. You cannot get that time back. Once it's gone, it's gone, forever!

If your mom or dad is still in your life, love them. Love is an action word, so you have to show them that you love them by taking care of them in any way that is appropriate for their current situation. I am not able to take care of my parents physically, but I pray for their spirits to be at rest, at peace all the time. My heart weeps for them often. I enjoy visits from them in my dreams every now and then. Those are super special! I wake up feeling like I just had a visit with them. They are not usually together when they visit, but it happens sometimes. Love your family now! Call them. Text them. Visit them. Send a card. Do whatever you can for the people in your life to know without a shadow of a doubt that you love them with all your heart and everything that is in you! Go! Do it now!

Time is not on our side. If you pay attention, the days are going by really fast, and loved ones are leaving us every single day. I know we all get busy with our own lives, but do what you have to do to not live with regrets. You cannot get that time back once it's gone. GOD loves you, and He wants you to love one another. Follow His direction, and it will lead you back to Him one day. I am grateful for the time I had with my parents. We have forgiven one another for the past and are focusing on the moment when we are reunited. Thank you, Heavenly Father, for bringing me through some hard times. I know You have my back through it all. It's like Yolanda Adams says, "This battle is not yours. It's the Lord's." Glory hallelujah!

Does My Special Someone Exist?

But *GOD* commandeth His *love* toward us,
In that, while we were yet sinners,
Christ died for us.

—Romans 5:8

To be young and in love, how wonderful! All I ever wanted as a child was to grow up and marry the love of my life, my king. I dreamed of my knight in shining armor quite often as a young girl. I continued to dream of him as a teenager and thought I met him when I was nineteen.

We met at Kings Dominion of all places, and after that, we were inseparable. We started dating immediately after we returned from our perspective trips to the adventure park. He made me laugh. He made my heart smile. After a year of dating, he asked me to move in with him at his parents' house. I did. It was great! We were together two years when he proposed to me at Christmastime, and we were going to get married the next. "Were" being the operative word in that sentence.

What happened? Well, we were saving up for the wedding, I was anyway. I let him know that in no uncertain terms was I paying for this by myself. We had an account we were supposed to add to with each paycheck. That was the beginning of the decline. I'm busy saving and planning a wedding that just was not going to happen. Remember those red flags?

So the non-deposits was one red flag. The hanging out and getting high was the second. By the third red flag, I had my own apartment and moved out. By the way, the third red flag was that he cheated on me and they were having a baby. Blew my mind! I was done! He tried to convince me to stay with him, but there was no way I could do that after what he did. Oh! I lost the engagement ring, which was another red flag. Although I found out later that the ring had been stolen, not lost. It didn't matter, the relationship was over!

The next serious relationship (on my part) was with a very handsome young man who would become the father of my one and only child. We met at my new apartment complex in the early nineties. I was doing my laundry one evening after work, and he was coming in from work or somewhere else. Memory's a little foggy. We exchanged names and numbers. We already knew where the other lived, so exchanging addresses wasn't necessary. Our buildings were connected, and we lived basically next door to each other.

He and I became pretty hot and heavy soon after meeting. I had issues! I can admit that now. When you relate sex to love, you have some serious issues with mistaking lust for love. Anyway, we saw each other regularly for a while. We never really committed to a relationship. We were just having fun! I have to admit that I was catching feelings for him. He was beautiful and knew how to make me…let's just say smile. Laughing my fanny off!

I should have known that he was just too good to be true. We were on and off after a few months. I'm trying to remember if he moved out before I did, but that's not really important. I moved out after my mom transitioned to the next phase in this thing we call life. I also headed to Sumter, South Carolina, to fulfill my dream of becoming a teacher. I moved my things to my sister's place while I was away at school.

I would come home to visit during my school breaks, and he and I would hook up. Still nothing serious or official. We just enjoyed each other's company. I was home for winter break after my first semester at Morris College. (Dean's List, baby!) He called or I called. We hooked up and that was that! So back on campus in mid-January of the following year, I'm looking for my cycle to start. There was some spotting and nothing else for the next nine months because clearly there was a baby growing inside of me!

Guess who's pregnant? *What?* I had no idea how I was about to tell this man who is not really my boyfriend or significant other that I was pregnant with his child! I knew I was going to keep her as soon as I knew she was there. However, I needed to find out how he felt about the little life that was developing into a little human being. I could not call him and tell him over the phone. Instead, I wrote him a long letter, about three pages long or maybe more, that's not important.

I was just hanging out in the dorm one day, and I got a phone call. He got the letter and wanted to talk about what we were going to do. There was really nothing to talk about because I had already decided that I was keeping my baby. The way things were going in my life, I was not sure if I would ever have children. So it did not matter to me what he wanted to do at this point. I just lost my mother, and GOD has sent me this little angel to pour my love into. Of course, it took me a minute to come to that realization, but I was happy with my decision and still am almost twenty-three years later.

He and I are not together. There is no communication between us and very little between the two of them. We tried, or at least I thought we were trying, when I moved back to DC. There was a night when he came to pick up our daughter and me to spend the night with him. We went to his apartment, and he was cooking dinner for us. It felt like a real family at that very moment. Boy how quickly things change!

I was sitting in the living room, watching television with my baby girl, and there was a pounding at the door. I will not go into too much detail because this story is not about him and her. Let me just say I found out that he had another baby on the way, which meant he was sleeping with someone else unprotected. That was the beginning of the end of all hope for us to be the family I dreamed of having one day. I had to get out of that situation because there was just too much craziness going on with his new baby mama drama. I saw something in him that night that scared me, and I could no longer be involved or put myself in harm's way. It was over.

There were other relationships that came and went after that one, but none of them lasted nor are they even worth going into detail about. I was set free after this one relationship I thought would lead to marriage but ended with me walking away after being lied to for years. And just when you stop looking for Mr. Right, the Lord blesses you with the love of your life (outside of my child). I told myself that I was done with men for a while. I wanted to focus on me. But how many of you know that it's never our plan, it's GOD's plan?

We met during professional development at my very first school. He and his partner led our staff through a program that helped us relieve some stress. It was so different from the other training that we had in the past. We were all engaged and smiling by the end of it. I returned to my classroom to tidy up a bit and prepare some upcoming lessons. I had expressed to my grade level teammate that I thought one of the presenters was *fine*! I felt like a high schooler with a crush on the quarterback. It was hilarious!

Well, the next thing we know is I'm being paged in my classroom from the office. A colleague informed me that one of the presenters (Mr. *Fine*!) would like to speak with me and for me to come down to the office. I played it cool, that is, until she disconnected. I ran to the other classroom and told my partner-teacher that he wanted to see me downstairs. I was losing my cool like some high school teenager!

As I was coming down the stairs, I could see him standing at the end of the hall outside the office. I was blushing and found it hard to look him in the face. I went into the office like I didn't know who wanted to see me and spoke with my colleague. I went back into the hall where he was, and we introduced ourselves. We talked for a little bit, and he gave me his number. So the ball was in my court. If I was interested, I would have to call him, which I did. I cannot even front, I was definitely interested.

We went out to dinner three days later, and we've been together ever since. It's now more than fourteen years later! GOD knew what I needed and arranged that meeting between the two of us. I had given up to tell you the truth. I just thought I was supposed to be by myself, and I was good with that.

It is my testimony that if we just wait on GOD, if we just step to the side and let Him work, our lives will be blessed beyond our wildest dreams. I have dreamed of having my own family since I was a little girl. I went through the valleys of boyfriends, bedmates, and the sort to learn what I did not want in a relationship. We have to recognize that we go through certain things in our lives to learn some valuable lessons, as well as to serve as an example of how to overcome some serious valley lows. We also put ourselves through situations that could have been avoided if we only listened to that still small voice that was telling us to do otherwise. My GOD, the things I could have avoided if I had only listened. I am grateful that GOD's mercy was with me through it all because He knew I deserved better.

I thought this man was my champion. A man who had always been on my side, by my side no matter what I threw his way. I know I have not been the best helpmate, but with GOD's love, I am learning how to let go and trust. It has been a long road, and it just got a little longer. This man whom I thought was the one, the end-all and be all, is still talking to this woman he met years ago whom he claimed was just a business associate. Well, I may have been born on a Tuesday, but not this Tuesday! I saw some e-mails from 2017 to the present, so there's no denying it. I knew I did not trust him for a good reason! It's over, and it has been for quite some time. He is not the man, the king I thought he was! He just proved how untrustworthy some men can be no matter what they say out of their mouths. There have been a slew of other signs that let me know that he was not the one, and I'm finally ready to accept them and move on.

I'm so happy that GOD is working on me and helping me to lock into my intuition. I am crying out to GOD at this moment to send the man He created just for me! I need GOD, and I call on Him every day, all day, because I need His glory, His grace, and His mercy. I thank You for the way You love me and care for me, better than I care for myself. Lord, I praise Your Holy Name, and I want more of Your Spirit in my life. Thank You for bringing me to this day and causing me to see this man for the wolf in sheep's clothing that he is and has always been. He was never mine, but he was sent to teach me a valuable lesson. The lesson is to trust my gut, trust my instinct!

If it growls like a wolf, howls like a wolf, then it's a darn wolf! I am taking a few steps back and allowing myself time to heal and grow. It's time that I take care of myself. Whatever GOD has for me, it is for me and will find its way to me at the right time! Whew! Give me strength! Praise GOD!

The Love of My Life

I write unto you, little *children* because your
sins are forgiven you for His name's sake.

—1 John 2:12

My daughter knows that I am writing a book, but she has no idea how big of a part of my life she has played. I thought I would never have any children. I had a tumor removed along with my right ovary when I was only nineteen years old. I let go of the idea of being a mother right then. I was sad about that, but I figured I would be the best auntie ever to my nieces and nephews. That was good enough for me! Or so I thought.

Well, let me tell you this, it is never your plan! You read earlier about my discovery of my pregnancy and having to share it with her father so there's no need to rehash that situation again.

What I want to share is the awesomeness of carrying her and how wonderful it felt to be a mom. I remember the first time I felt her move inside of me. I was away at school, of course, and lying on my bed in my dorm room. All of a sudden, I felt this little flutter. I jumped up and placed my hands on my tummy, which was starting to protrude. I wanted to feel that flutter again. I was so excited, it moved me to tears.

I couldn't believe I was going to be someone's mother. I cried so many days and nights because I knew I wouldn't have my mom there to help me raise this child. I had only told a few people at school and in my family that I was expecting. I just wanted to enjoy being pregnant without any stress. I must say that my pregnancy was pretty good for the most part. There was heartburn and two episodes of vomiting. I also could not stand the smell of most things.

I moved to Savannah after school let out in May of 1995 and stayed with my brother, his wife, and their children. I loved being in Savannah during my pregnancy because I was born there, and my daughter would also be a Georgia peach. I was close to my maternal grandmother and both sides of my family. My mom was buried in Savannah, so I could visit her gravesite whenever I wanted to with a ride from someone.

The day I went into labor, I had just eaten a delicious dinner made by my sister-in-law. We had pork chops, green beans, and rice with gravy. I ate everything on my plate. But that wasn't enough. There I was, big as I could be, and I saw the pizza my nieces and nephews were eating and decided to take a slice. Well, I went to bite into that slice and felt something happening down below. I stopped before I could even take a bite and said to my family, "If I'm not mistaken, I'm in labor."

Calmly, I went to the bathroom to check things out and saw it. The mucus plug had come out and my water was breaking. I walked back toward everyone and calmly stated, "Yes, it's time." They all became very excited! I was wearing white jean shorts (imagine that). My sister-in-law went to the car to take me to the hospital, and I was going to the linen closet to get a towel to sit on so I wouldn't get the seats all wet. She was like, "Nobody cares about that. Let's go!"

Let me tell you that we arrived at that hospital in eight minutes flat. It was too funny. She was blowing her horn and speeding the whole way. I couldn't laugh then but afterward, and even as I reflect on it now, I cannot help but laugh. She is no longer with us, and I miss her every day, but we had so many laughs about that day.

So we got there around 7:45 p.m. on a Friday evening, and they put me in a wheelchair, got me all checked in, and took me to my room. This room was beautiful! It was like a hotel room. I couldn't believe how nice the room was, but I was in so much pain by then that I could only say it to myself. I will skip the part about what happened when they asked me if I had eaten anything prior to going into labor.

They put me on the bed to check my cervix, and I had only dilated 1.5 centimeters. What? With all the pain, I just knew I was further along than that, but that was it. Hours go by and the contractions were strong. They checked again, and I was about three centimeters. Now the contractions were getting stronger, and the pain was great. I was trying to be strong because I wanted a natural birth. Let me tell you, when that pain is kicking your butt the way it was with me, you quickly give in to that epidural.

Wow! What a difference that made! I was feeling no pain and felt like I was floating in the clouds. I could not eat anything but ice chips, which I did in abundance. I was able to relax and watch television. Although the contractions continued, I did not feel a thing.

My cervix continued to take its time opening. I may have had two hours of sleep before the epidural wore off and got a second dose just in time because those pains were rushing back. Well, it was after midnight, and not much progress was happening down there. I started to worry. Thankfully, my sister and sister-in-law were there to keep me calm.

It was morning, and the sun was coming up, but still no baby. She was in there chilling! I talked to her and let her know that I understand that it's nice and warm in there, but it's time to come out so we can meet face-to-face. I was six or seven centimeters. This was taking forever! I was tired, my body was in a lot of pain, and this baby did not want to come out! Now the epidural was wearing off, and it's too late to get any more. So it looked like we were going natural!

So after more than sixteen hours of active labor, we were finally ready to push. By this time, I was too exhausted! This little person inside of me did not seem to want to come out, and I didn't have the energy to push her out. I pushed a few times and couldn't do it again. The doctor had my sister and my sister-in-law hold hands crisscross over my belly, and on the next contraction, they would push down as I pushed as best I could. What do you know? Seventeen hours and fifteen minutes after I entered the hospital, my pumpkin pooh was here. It worked!

My beautiful baby girl was finally here and healthy although a little jaundiced. I cried. She cried. The nurses swooped her up and away to check her out and clean her off. I told my sisters to go count her fingers and toes and make sure she was good. I was not able to hold her right away because they had to change the sheets on my bed and clean me up as well. We made quite a mess bringing this little one into the world.

Once I was back in the bed, they brought her to me, and I cried some more as I looked at this little person's face. She was beautiful! I had waited nine months to meet this little one that had been pulling on the navel cord most of my pregnancy. At that moment, I was the happiest I had ever been in my entire life. I was so glad to hold her in my arms and look at that little face! She had a head full of hair and was as cute as a button! I was head over heels in love!

We went home a few days later after I broke a fever I had spiked after giving birth. She came home with a special blue light to help get rid of jaundice and earned the nickname glow-worm from her uncle. None of that mattered to me. I was just happy to finally be able to hold her and see her little face. I believe I was in love for the very first time. This little girl stole my heart and still has it to this day. She is my one and only child. I cannot imagine my life without her. She has my heart forever and always!

We moved back to DC when she was a few months old and moved in with my youngest sister who had two girls of her own. It wasn't the best living arrangement, but we made it work. I loved being there with my sister and nieces. I was grateful that my daughter would grow up with her cousins and build a close bond. My sister is the best, and we moved into a townhouse when my daughter was just about to start kindergarten.

I was in school and graduating in the spring. Life was good. Or so I thought. There were thoughts of suicide even then. I could not snap myself out of it. I was enjoying watching my daughter and my nieces grow up and do well in school. I was about to live my dream as a teacher. Depression didn't care. It crept in, but I was really good at hiding it by then. I smiled and wore the mask.

When those bad thoughts would come to mind, I would think about my beautiful little girl and what it would do to her if I harmed myself. She saved my life, time and again. I could never leave her with that vision or those bad feelings of guilt. I want her to know that my depression and anxiety has nothing to do with her. She has done nothing but bring great joy into my life.

I believe with all my heart that GOD blessed me with this gift because He knew I would never do anything to hurt this child that He placed in my care. And I have to say He was right. I have so much love for her and want her to have the life she deserves. I could never do anything to jeopardize that. I would not be able to forgive myself.

I truly believe in the old adage that everything happens for a reason. GOD does not make mistakes nor does He miss an opportunity to teach us something. GOD gave me the blessing of my daughter even though I thought I could not have children to give me a reason to live. That's exactly what she is to me, my reason for living even to this day.

Anyone who knows me knows that I would do absolutely anything for my little girl even though she's grown now. She will always be my little girl. GOD knows the pain I've been in all these years. He knew I was ready to throw it all away because I didn't have the husband and family I thought I was supposed to have by that time. I wanted my life to be like the dream I had as a little girl, and it wasn't.

I was giving up. I lost my mother at a very important moment in my life, our lives. We were finally having the relationship I wanted with her as a little girl. Then, all of a sudden, she was gone. I was hurting. I wanted out! But on September 9, 1995, at 12:15 p.m., GOD sent me an angel. The absolute love of my life!

What I want you to know is that even in moments of weakness, GOD will strengthen you. GOD will draw near to you and show you exactly who He is when you're in doubt. I give Him all the glory for trusting me with the life of another. I praise GOD for the lifeline He threw me in the hardest time of my life. My beautiful daughter is the angel I needed to save my life.

I will forever worship GOD for the blessings in my life but none more important than my daughter, Tatyana. I hope she understands that because of my love for her and the Highest, I want to be here to share life with her. I pray that she will find the peace she needs in her life as well. It is my hope and prayer that she will look at my life as an example of how things can turn around when you believe in the Highest.

Thank You, GOD, for the blessing of my daughter! I am so honored and grateful to be her mom. May she receive the blessings that You have for her and only her. May she use those blessings to help others and serve You. Praise GOD! I love you, Mommie!

Instant Family

Of whom the whole *family* in heaven and earth is named,
That he would grant you, according to the riches of his glory, to be
Strengthened with might by his Spirit in the inner man.

—Ephesians 3:15–16

My siblings and I unexpectedly lost our mother in May of 1994. This changed my life immediately. I was in my twenties, but I still needed my mother. I don't know how many of you have experienced this life-changing moment, and I'm not sure how you felt afterward. However, for me, I felt like an orphan, like a child without any parents even though my father was still living. He wasn't that involved in our lives. Although he did step up after her passing. Only GOD has been able to help me through that most painful part of my life. I'm still learning how to deal with it. It gets easier, but it never goes away.

In June of 1996, my youngest sister and I began receiving lessons from two missionaries of the Church of Jesus Christ of Latter-Day Saints. They found me when I was still out in the world just living, studying for my bachelor of arts in education, and raising my beautiful daughter. At the time, my sister and I were living together with our daughters. We were expecting company when there was a knock at the door. Thinking it was who we were expecting, we opened the door without hesitation. Well, to our surprise, it was two elders from the church.

Hindsight being 20/20, I know now exactly why this blindsided meeting took place. The elders were and are two of the nicest people I have ever met. They not only taught us about the Book of Mormon and the teachings of Jesus Christ, but they became an important part of our family. They also provided us with the opportunity to raise our girls in the church. We, my sister and I, were baptized into the church on June 16.

We started attending the church weekly and participating in several activities that happened during the weeks. The girls, my sister, and I were all welcomed with open arms by all the members.

There was one in particular family that we bonded with instantly, the Wilson family. This was a husband and wife with four children. Brother Wilson had this bigger than life personality and was so sweet. He was the only one my daughter would let throw her up into the air and catch. If anyone else dared try to do this same thing, she would have a fit. You would often see her in his arms or sitting on his lap during our sacrament meetings. She was totally spoiled by him.

Sister Wilson was and still is the other mother GOD sent to us. She welcomed us into their lives without hesitation. We quickly bonded and began hanging out with them outside of the church. We would have family home evenings with them, they picked us up for church, which was quite funny because there was not much room for all of us. We would pack in that car like sardines, but it was funny and endearing. They loved us like we had known them all our lives.

We became a family in every sense of the word. They unofficially adopted us as their godchildren. Godchildren. I had never thought about that word as much as I do today. It means to me that our chance meeting with the elders of the church was not by chance but divine intervention for our GOD. We were supposed to meet the elders and join this wonderful church in order to meet the other part of our family. What I know for sure is that GOD does not make mistakes and coincidences are not just coincidences, but purposeful incidents that lead you to your destiny.

We, unfortunately, had to bid a fond farewell to Brother Wilson in 1999, but he is still the father GOD sent to us to touch our lives, our hearts, and our souls. He even touched our taste buds. I forgot to mention how he was well-known in the church as the Candy Man because he would often be found with a big bag of candy to give out to the children, young and young at heart. We love him and miss him every day!

Sister Wilson, or Mama (as I affectionately refer to her), and the rest of our instant family is still together for all those important celebrations. We are family in every sense of the word. Families are not cookie-cutter. They are specially made by people who truly love and care about one another and that's us. I love each and every one of my god-relatives like they're my natural-born relatives.

I am so grateful that GOD sent the other members of my family to us, not to replace our mom, but to show us how He would never leave us nor forsake us in our times of need. My GOD, our GOD is awesome, and He will always answer your prayers! It may not be in the neat little package you were expecting, but I promise it will be exactly what you need at that particular moment. It may be a hundred times better!

Praise GOD through your mountain highs and valley lows, and GOD will show up and show out in your life more than you could ever imagine.

This chapter is dedicated in loving memory to my godfather, the Candy Man, Brother Carlton Wilson. Gone but not forgotten. May your spirit continue to rest in peace. I love you with my whole heart!

Overcoming the Enemy

Blessed are the merciful:
for they shall obtain *mercy*.

—Matthew 5:7

As I am writing and reflecting on my life, I am reminded of the adversary often. My faith in GOD has grown over the years. However, I feel like I have been fighting my way through every step of the way to get to where I am today. The enemy is busy and always making attempts to steal your soul. I know because I have struggled with the thought of throwing up my hands and just giving in to it.

I am not sure when and where it started exactly, but I have been dealing with anxiety and depression for some years now. I believe it has been an obstacle since I was eight or nine years old. It feels good to say that out loud and to share it with you today because I have worked hard to hide it for much too long. I was embarrassed, ashamed, and afraid to admit that I have a mental health issue. I did not want people looking at me as if I was some ticking time bomb waiting to go off.

I know there are many out there that just thought I was mean and cold. This couldn't be further from the truth of the person that I truly am. I built a fortress around me years ago and know now that I have been knocking it down brick by brick slowly but surely. I am not that person that others experienced. I am a loving, generous person. Unfortunately, I was trapped inside of the little girl who had been hurt by so many for so long that I acted out of anger and caused pain to others. Please forgive me for I knew not what I was doing.

I want everyone out there to be happy by truly discovering that spiritual being you were before you came to this sinful world. This is the essence of who we all are and why we should not judge one another by the packaging our souls arrived in. We must understand that this is all a part of the tests that we go through during our time here. This is only one phase of our lives. It is my belief that we continue to live in the spirit world after we have run our race on earth.

I can remember when I was still in the dating world and how I thought I had to have a man in my life for my life to mean anything. I was just out there living and being very promiscuous. I was selective in the men I slept with, but I was not trying to fall in love with any of them. The ones I thought I was in love with ended up hurting me the most. I started having thoughts of suicide at an early age. I mean, I was seriously contemplating it! I would plan it out down to who would find my body.

Depression is horrible! I am fighting it every minute of every day because I know that no matter how sad, how low I feel, GOD loves me. GOD refuses to give up on me and won't allow me to give up on myself or give in to the adversary. GOD is love and the love of GOD lives inside of me. It lives inside of all of us. We have to remind ourselves of this daily to build our strength and testimony of the one and only true GOD.

In June and early July 2018, I had thoughts of suicide because I lost my job and have found it difficult to find anything else. I have a nonprofit that I cannot seem to get off the ground or find the financial support it needs to provide the community outreach I want to give to the youth. I just want to stop the pain, the misery I'm experiencing daily. People have no idea how bad this is unless they have gone through it themselves. It is the worst thing I have ever experienced.

You feel so alone. You think no one can help you. You believe life will only get worse the longer your breathing. There is no hope! You can't see the light at the end of the tunnel. It's completely dark! You only see things that are devastating and negative. You believe you deserve to die because you're a failure. You can't see any way out of this black hole. You start to fall deeper and deeper into it.

There are days when I won't eat and don't even care if I eat. I want to stay in bed and do absolutely nothing. When I watch television, I do everything I can to avoid commercials about depression and anxiety. I cry when I hear stories of others dealing with or overcoming depression. I want to be someone that overcomes this horrible illness. I hope this book shines a much-needed light on it so no one else has to go through this and feel like they can't talk about it because of the stigma society has put on mental illness.

You should know to never tell a person showing signs of depression and anxiety to "let it go" or "everything's going to be okay." This is not what we need to hear. We need our loved ones to encourage us to talk to professionals. It's like a person addicted to drugs, you can lead them to rehab, but you can't make them stay. The same is true for people struggling with depression if anyone recognizes the symptoms. Some of us become very good at hiding our true feelings most of the time. I am one of those people. How many of my family members or friends asked me about being depressed? None. How many suspect that I am depressed or anxious? I don't know, but I do know that none of them have approached me about seeking help for it.

I realize as I am writing and sharing my life of testimonies with you that this is saving my life! I understand that I have been trying to battle this monster on my own like it was just going to go away. I accept that I cannot do this alone. I need the support of my family and a highly skilled professional to help me control this beast that has controlled me for a great portion of my life. I want to be in control of my healing, but I know I need my Heavenly Father to help me. So I'm throwing up my hands and asking to be saved from myself.

GOD is my strength and all of my health comes from Him. GOD is the one that has been the common denominator in my life all along. I was just too stubborn and too lost to realize it or accept it. He has been waiting for me all this time. I know now that my depression started the first time I kept something horrible that happened to me to myself. I locked it away and started that fortress around my heart, my life. I was going to take all the ugliness, the hurt, and the misery to my grave. But GOD!

GOD is telling me that I don't have to do that. I can live the life I want, and it starts with freeing myself and giving myself permission to live. My oh my, GOD is good! Writing this chapter has done something for me that I was not at all expecting. I am going to make the call to find someone I can talk to about what I'm going through. This is why I love my GOD! All things have a purpose in your life, and this book, this chapter, is inspiring me to stay in the game and use my life to help someone else.

I want to thank GOD for using me and allowing me to finally open my eyes to see that the key to my salvation has been inside of me all along. Please seek the help you need no matter what may be ailing you. Do not sit idly by and allow the enemy to mislead you and have you believing that you don't deserve to win. You are a child of GOD as am I, and we deserve to have a life filled with the blessings GOD promised Abraham centuries ago. I am in counseling now and receiving the support I need to have a healthy mind. I want to be a complete person, and I now feel that I am on the road to being the person I was truly created to be. My testimonies of the goodness of GOD are growing every minute. I love you, and GOD loves you too! Keep your head up!

Finding and Loving Me

Now *faith* is the substance of things hoped for,
the evidence of things not seen.

—Hebrews 11:1

It amazes me to look back on my life and see how far I have come. I was made to feel uncomfortable in my own skin for so long by outside sources. I allowed the enemy to get into my psyche and destroy me. What did I know? I was a child when it all started. It's no wonder I went through the boys and men as I did. I didn't love myself. I didn't believe I deserved to be loved. I know now that I was punishing myself. I was broken. My heart, my spirit, all of me was just broken.

I held all the hurt, the disappointment, the ugliness close to my heart, and it consumed me. I had no idea that life could be any other way. I thought this would be my life until I left this world. There were many dark nights when I just wanted it to be over. I asked GOD to take me, but instead, He continued to wake me up each day. Then I started thinking that He was punishing me. Why else would He keep me here to feel so much pain?

For so long, I hid my true feelings behind a mask. I lost myself. I was not living but going through the motions of life. I allowed others to mistreat me, lie to me, cheat on me, and use me for their own selfish needs. There were some mountain highs in my life, but those valley lows nearly took me away from this place. I didn't even care! I just thought the pain would stop if I died.

When you have low self-esteem, self-hatred, and a broken spirit, you want nothing more than for that pain to go away by any means necessary. I was crying out for someone, something to save me from myself. I was on a path to self-destruction. I went to church and tried to fill my soul with the goodness of GOD as a young adult. I still went home and thought about how I could kill myself. I would plan it all out as I mentioned earlier. I was on the edge, and at any given moment, I was jumping off.

I know my family and friends will read this and wonder if they saw signs of my depression. I believe I was pretty good at wearing the mask and not showing how desperate I was to be saved from the horrible thoughts in my head. I would look in the mirror at times and not recognize the person looking back at me. I would sometimes see that little girl where it all started. She was so sad! It broke my heart to see how sad she looked. She just wanted me to save her, and I didn't have a clue how to do that. I blamed myself for so much of the pain. I am so sorry for holding on to the pain and not being able to let it go until now.

This book is giving me the opportunity to release and purge all the bad feelings, bad experiences I went through as a child and young adult. This is not easy to do, but it is necessary for my healing, our healing. GOD has our backs and will not let us fail this time. It's time to take it all to the altar and leave it there. I know now that I held on to the little girl inside of me because she was familiar, and I felt safe with her. However, if I'm going to be my best self, I have to let her go. It's time for me to stand up, forgive myself, and love myself.

GOD created me in His image for a purpose, and I want to live out that purpose. I have always wanted to be a teacher and believe that was a calling placed on my life before I was even a zygote. Teaching comes in many forms, and I believe my testimonies are lessons for others to learn from as is their testimonies for me to learn from. I know GOD is my Biggest Fan because I'm still here to share my stories, my testimonies of His grace and mercy with you today.

I am learning how to love and forgive myself more and more each day. It is not an easy process especially after more than forty years of the opposite, but I have put my trust in GOD that I will be healed and made whole. GOD has not let me down or let me go after everything I have been through, and I know He is not going to let me go now. I am feeling stronger as I release these words on to the pages.

It is my belief that as the words on these pages are read by people who are seeking inspiration, it will cause healing in your lives. Please know that you are enough, more than enough when it comes to our Heavenly Father. GOD loves us unconditionally, and He wants us to love one another the same way. So, brothers and sisters, it is my testimony that grace and mercy from the Almighty GOD within each of us is yours today and always. Grace and mercy have been my best friends for more than forty-nine years and will be there every step of the way from here on out.

Thank you for picking up this book and allowing my story, the good, the bad, and the ugly to inspire and touch your spirit. It is my hope that you read a passage from my life and use it to stand on, to cherish the life you have been given. I am but a servant of the Highest, and it is my honor to serve as a source of inspiration to my sisters and brothers around the globe. You can do this! I believe in you, and I know that if you give GOD a chance He will lead you out of whatever you're going through. GOD loves you, and so do I! Peace and blessings to one and all!

Sometimes You Need a Push

And He said unto me, My *grace* is sufficient for thee:
For My strength is made perfect in weakness.
Most gladly therefore will I rather glory in my infirmities,
That the power of Christ may rest upon me.

—2 Corinthians 12:9

How many times have you felt the prompting of the Spirit to do something and ignored it? I have done this on too many occasions to count. Although there have been several times when I did listen to and obey the loving guidance of GOD. No matter how many times you ignore or do not heed the call, GOD will continue to push you in the direction of your purpose.

What GOD has for me is for me, and so it is with everyone else. Trust and believe me that GOD will have His way and guide your footsteps along the path that has been prepared for you long before you were even born. This is what I'm learning with every passing moment over the past two-plus years.

When you go to bed dreaming about the same thing over and over again, you realize GOD is trying to tell you something. Because we are human beings, we forget or often neglect that spiritual part of ourselves. Because there are bills to be paid and others to take care of, we also forget about ourselves. It is not easy to let go of the familiar for something that has been just a dream for so long.

Someone I love dearly gave me the mantra, "Control what you can control." It's not always so simple to just let go of something you think you control to reach out for the thing you have desired within your heart for years. Relinquishing control is never easy, but it is necessary.

I want nothing more but to reach back into the communities I have grown up in to help the young people living in poverty just as I did as a child. I want to equip them with the things they need to be a well-rounded, contributing citizen of this world. I never had anyone that I could turn to for emotional or financial support. If I wanted something, like my cheerleader uniform, I had to work and pay for it myself.

GOD doesn't want to see His children suffer. He wants us to love one another and be in service to one another. This is why I had the recurring dream of my non-profit. It would not stop. So when the middle school I was working in closed, I seriously considered starting it. Pause! How would you pay the bills? What would you do for health insurance? Just a couple of the questions I asked myself. Push!

I was offered a job with a former supervisor and coworker that I could not refuse. I absolutely loved it! I worked with people I loved and the students I loved no matter how much they fought against the new systems that were put in place to make things better for them. We fought long and hard to keep this school up and running, but there is an adversary who cares less about the children and more about statistics. Another push!

Even though the papers were filed and the non-profit was up and running, this was only on paper. I thought I was ready and able to start this foundation. However, there are always those seeds of doubt that cloud your mind. There's also the bills that never stop. Another job and year go by with the attempt to operate the foundation part-time. Push again!

Months go by with little to no support of the foundation and no leads on a new place of employment, even temporary. I would rather be broke if I could dedicate my time to serving our youth. If it were only about me, that's exactly what I would have done. I had to put another pin in my dream. Of course, I found another job before the year ended because GOD is so awesome.

Six months go by, and I'm blindsided and released from my job. Wow! Depression and anxiety about bills emerge. How much more can I take? I was ready to throw in the towel and just give up on everything. But GOD. Push!

That last push landed me right here in the midst of writing my very first book. After all this time has passed, I finally understand that this is exactly what GOD was pushing me toward. I kept thinking it was about my dream of the non-profit, but it was this book. When I went away to college, I was initially studying English to become an English teacher and writer.

GOD has mysterious ways of letting us know who's in charge. I finally get it. I am so grateful that He has been with me every step of the way and brought me to this moment. This book has unlocked so much for me and has given me the power needed to finally let go of that hurt little girl. Sometimes you need a few nudges in the right direction followed by the big push that grabs your attention. I thank Thee, O Lord, for the push to let go of the past and let GOD have His way with my life.

GOD's Love Is the Prize

(an original poem)

My past held me hostage for so many years
The devil, not my past, did this to me
For my past made me strong
To see through the tears.

GOD is my strength, my Lord, and my Light
When I thought I was done and couldn't go on
Heavenly Father sent His heavenly angels to fight
And because I believed, I'm still here, I won.

So many days, minutes passed, I counted the hours
I was ready and willing to surrender my powers
But the GOD I serve and continuously praise said
"Don't give up, my child, for there are better days ahead!"

GOD's grace and mercy were there through it all
They knew it was not easy and never let me fall
I put my trust in them to help me through
And I'm still here today to now inspire you.

I'm not perfect, and my journey isn't over
My faith is in GOD and not some four-leaf clover
So if you just give Him a mustard-seed chance
You will smile again and gain a brand-new dance.

GOD IS MY BIGGEST FAN

I know GOD can pull you through
My life is the living proof
It's time to stand up and claim what's yours
You're a child of the Highest, not here for a tour.

Love one another is the commandment He gave
It's not just a saying but how your life can be saved
Come on! I know you can do it!
GOD is your biggest fan too, and He will help you through it!

People often think they know someone really well
Walk a mile in their shoes, then you can tell
Your life isn't as hard as you thought
The fights you won were because GOD fought.

What others have gone through gets covered by the mask
And keeping up appearances is a strenuous task
We don't tell the truth because then you'll judge
Our perfect will somehow be blemished and smudged.

Stop caring about what other people think of you
Put GOD first in your life and watch the wonders He can do
I've had to learn the hard way that my life is not my own
It belongs to the Heavenly Father and Christ alone.

Throw up your hands and surrender it all
For GOD is trying to tell you something so answer the call
You deserve so much more than the eyes can see
Just give it to the Lord and watch it change so graciously
GOD is pushing me toward my purpose, passion, and dreams
I have to stop fighting the inevitable and trust of the Most Supreme
Do not worry when people look at you
with such judgment in their eyes
Know deep in your heart and soul that GOD's love is the prize.

Heartfelt Gratitude

It is a good thing to give *thanks*
unto the LORD, and to sing *praises* unto
Thy name, O most High.

—Psalm 92:1

As I close out the last chapter of my very first book, I want to express my gratefulness to GOD for His grace and mercy upon my life, my heart, and my soul. I want you to understand that this was not an easy project to complete. Like the birth of my daughter, this was a labor of love.

I am not the kind of person who shares her innermost thoughts and feelings. I know how to keep a secret and was planning to take all this to the grave. I would have never been able to do this without the Great Redeemer! What I have shared with you are the deepest wounds of my life and some of the happiest moments of my life.

I decided to write this book because I wanted to free myself from the guilt and shame the adversary places in our lives to cause doubt and every negative thing to keep us from the great love of GOD. It was never mine, but I held on to it out of fear and embarrassment. I share these speed bumps of my life in order to help someone else. This year has been deemed as the year of the woman after so many stories of sexual harassment and sexual misconduct have come forth out of Hollywood, the world of sports, and even the military.

Those stories have given me strength and courage. I chose not to name my violators because I have asked GOD to help me forgive them and forgive myself for taking responsibility for something that was not my fault. I just want my life back. I want to be able to live without this holding me back from living my true purpose.

While the testimonies of the brave women and even one man, that I know of, touched my life in a mighty way, I want to pay it forward and do the same for someone else out there who may be scared to tell their family about the struggles they may be facing. It may be depression, anxiety, or sexual molestation. Whatever it is, I want them to know that they are not alone. I punished myself for years by not owning my truth and standing up against all of it. I allowed the enemy to have control of my life. No more!

I lost my maternal grandmother thirteen days before she was to turn ninety-three. She would have encouraged me years ago to seek professional help to have a healthy mind I deserved. She was the best, and I miss her every single day. More than ever, I feel her presence along with the presence of my other guardian angels I call Mom and Dad. This is why I know now is the time for it all. Now is all we have. Tomorrow is not promised to any of us. So whatever dreams you may have, whatever goals are on your bucket list, get to it now. You deserve it, and besides, it may lead you to your purpose. Stand up and take back your life! I stand with you! I stand for you! You are not alone.

The horrible things you have been through or are going through are not yours. We were never promised that it would be easy, but we were promised to not have to go through any of it on our own. Please speak with someone and let them know what is going on with you. There is someone out there who will listen to you and guide you in the direction of healing. Remember, this is not yours alone. GOD is there waiting for you to cry out to Him to help you. Trust and believe me that He will be there. This is His battle to fight! Let GOD come into your life and rid it of all the horrible things the devil has caused you to follow.

If no one else in your life is telling you that you are worth saving, let me be the first. You are worth saving! Let the Creator show you the path to healing and happiness! It's yours if you just cry out to Him! It's yours if you have faith and know that you can come out of this. You can! I have. It takes one step at a time, but I'm doing it! I have to do this because GOD deserves 100 percent of me because that is what I get every day.

May the GOD you serve and the testimonies of others give you the courage and strength to stand in your truth and be healed. Give yourself permission to live the life you have always dreamt of. You hold the key to unlock the desires of your heart. You can do it!

It is my hope and prayer that something I shared within these pages will bless your life in a mighty way.

This has never been about fame or fortune. This is my freedom cry! May you find the appropriate avenue to your own freedom and joy of living. Live your purpose! Find yourself in the service of others when you think your life cannot get any worse. You have more to give than you think. Please avoid the naysayers and social media trolls. You deserve happiness just as much as anyone else! Your key to happiness is locked inside of you. Find it and release the joy that is meant for you. Your happiness is your responsibility. I had to start a gratitude journal to remind me of all the wonderful blessings in my life. I could actually see that I have much more good in my life than I ever knew. I am blessed, and I know that my current situation was never meant to be my final destination. The same is true for you. Keep pushing, praying, and moving forward! Know that GOD abides in you and you in Him!

May the GOD I serve bless your life in a mighty way! Know as I do, I was created on purpose for a purpose!

Peace and love to you all!

About the Author

Sharon Wright is a mother, educator, writer, poet, and entrepreneur who lives in Washington, DC, with her daughter. She began writing poetry as a teenager and used it as a way to express her innermost feelings. She was a teacher for ten years with District of Columbia Public Schools and Public Charter Schools before becoming an administrator for the past nine years. *GOD Is My Biggest Fan* is her first book to be published. It is her hope that it's the first of many best-selling books in her collection.

CPSIA information can be obtained
at www.ICGtesting.com
Printed in the USA
BVHW031916190221
600640BV00022B/192